Canadian Gardening's
WATER
in the GARDEN

By JANET DAVIS

with LIZ PRIMEAU and THE EDITORS of CANADIAN GARDENING MAGAZINE

A FENN PUBLISHING COMPANY / MADISON PRESS BOOK

CANADIAN GARDENING'S

WATER *in the* GARDEN

ISBN 1-55168-282-6

A FENN PUBLISHING COMPANY / MADISON PRESS BOOK
First Published in 2005

FENN PUBLISHING COMPANY LTD.
Bolton, Ontario, Canada

Distributed in Canada by

H. B. FENN AND COMPANY LTD.
Bolton, Ontario, Canada, L7E 1W2
www.hbfenn.com

Produced by
MADISON PRESS BOOKS
1000 Yonge Street, Suite 200
Toronto, Ontario, Canada
M4W 2K2

Printed in Singapore

Introduction

Ponds and waterfalls used to be a privilege of the rich, but not any more. With today's submersible pumps and liners, anyone can make a water feature. My husband and I are living proof of this — we have two.

After we'd had a small, wood-framed pond sunk into our new deck, my husband confessed that what he'd really wanted was a natural-looking pond with a waterfall. "So I can hear the sound of water," he said.

He decided to make one himself. I came home to find him standing waist deep in an oval-shape hole in the ground, carefully fitting in PVC liner according to the instructions from a local pond-supply store. Soon he was adding a rock edging and a low waterfall. I offered to make a pebble beach, partly so birds could hop to the water's edge for a drink, and partly because I was afraid the pond might end up looking like ... well, a hole in the ground outlined with rocks.

The pond is now well established, and my husband is rightfully proud of it. We dine beside it on hot nights, enjoying the cooling sound of water cascading over the rocks. On summer mornings, the fish swim up to greet us, mouths open in expectation of breakfast.

As my husband says, anyone can make a pond — as long as he has some expert advice! In *Water in the Garden, Canadian Gardening's* experts take you through the process step by step, from deciding on the perfect location and style to installing a liner and choosing the right pump. You'll also find practical information on filters, fish, plants and winter care, plus great ideas for small water features to enliven the tiniest garden, balcony or terrace.

Liz Primeau, Editor
Canadian Gardening Magazine

CHAPTER ONE

CASTING *a* SPELL WITH WATER

A pond
or other water feature,
no matter how small, makes any
city garden or expansive country
property a little more romantic,
a lot more animated and
infinitely more interesting.

WATER *in a* GARDEN

Water can be incorporated in a garden in countless ways. A formal reflecting pool, its tranquil surface a mirror of clouds and sky, might echo the classic lines of a stately stone home — while a natural pond edged with irises and rushes, where goldfish swim lazily beneath elegant water lilies, is the perfect complement to an informal garden.

Well-designed and skillfully integrated swimming pools, lap pools, hot tubs or plunge pools — although not water gardens in the classic sense — also have wonderful reflective qualities. The best marry function with form, proving every bit as ornamental as the prettiest lily pond.

Water adds to the seasonal appeal of a garden. In spring, a pond becomes a breeding ground for tadpoles and a watering hole for migrating birds. In summer, even the smallest water feature offers a cooling oasis from the heat of the day. And as the gardening year draws to a close, water captures the colorful splendor of

A birdbath is a simple way to bring the reflective quality of water into the garden.

autumn and the stark beauty of the frozen winter landscape.

If still water pleases, moving water pleases even more. Whether it's the splash of a waterfall tumbling down stepped rocks in a hillside garden, the gentle burbling of a wet millstone or the musical cascade of an elaborate fountain, the sound of water enhances the feeling of tranquility within the garden while dulling the din of traffic and noise outside.

For gardeners with limited space or budgets, or for those who like the *idea* of water but don't necessarily want to bother with digging and maintaining a pond, there are several less ambitious options. For example, a wall fountain can be purchased as a ready-to-install kit. All you need to do is attach it to a fence or wall, fill its basin with water and plug in the recirculating pump (which draws the water up from the basin through flexible tubing into a spout in the upper part of the fountain). Voilà — the splash of water without a waterfall.

A bamboo water spout splashes gently into a partially buried container water garden, offering the calming sound of water while creating a distinctly Oriental mood.

Or, you can create a small pebble pool by arranging decorative river rocks or smooth pebbles on a grate above an underground reservoir (a preformed pond shell is ideal) containing water and a recirculating pump. The pump, which is plugged into an outdoor receptacle, is fitted with flexible tubing that carries water up through the rocks, allowing it to bubble over them before returning to the reservoir. This simple pool can be conjured on even a small deck or patio.

And then there are birdbaths; ceramic pots large enough to hold a miniature water lily; Japanese-inspired bamboo spouts; stone basins; and half whiskey barrels big enough for a few goldfish. (For more on other water features, see p. 84.)

The possibilities for introducing water into your garden are endless — as long as you remember to take the surroundings into account. Not every water feature is appropriate to every landscape. While birdbaths and basins will suit almost any garden, a waterfall or natural pond needs to be carefully planned and sensitively integrated.

By definition, of course, water gardening is inspired trickery. In the wild, a babbling brook doesn't start at the picket fence and come to a stop beside the garage. A natural waterfall tumbles down a rocky cliff because there's an immutable force of real, moving water at its back, not because there's a big recirculating pump at its base. And nature rarely plunks a wild pond in the middle of a tame lawn, surrounds it with petunias, fills it with a hodge-podge of aquatic plants and stocks it with a mini aquarium of fish and amphibians.

So how does the water gardener begin?

The answer is simple — by hiking along a mountain stream, walking through a natural marsh, sitting on a riverbank or on a dock beside a still northern lake. By going on garden tours, leafing through magazines, cutting out pictures and reading books like this one. And when all the research has been done, the wise gardener poses these two important questions: "What distinguishes my landscape? How can water, artificially introduced, enhance and improve it?"

Let's take a look at the way water has been incorporated in gardens throughout history. Then we'll help you discover the wonderful ways in which water can enhance and improve your own landscape.

Water Gardens
through the Ages

Decorative water features aren't new to gardens by any means. Villas in Pompeii, entombed by volcanic ash from Vesuvius in 79 A.D., were found to contain walled courtyard gardens, or peristyles, with pools and canals, some for catching rainwater from the roof. In ancient Persia, water was often featured in cruciform canals or in wall fountains with four symbolic water spouts — signifying the Persian belief in the four sacred rivers of life — that emptied into a basin below.

Baroque Italian Renaissance gardens, such as the Villa d'Este built in 1550, incorporated elaborate and often humorous water features, including cascading

stairways, spouting animal masks and even a hydraulically operated water organ that played music. In France, LeNotre's palatial gardens for Louis XIV at Versailles included the Parterre d'Eau, or water room, and numerous elaborate fountains. England's Romantic landscape movement of the 18th century introduced more naturalistic water features, typified by William Kent's famous 1738 design for Rousham Park, which included Venus's Vale — a cascading water course that spilled through a forested hillside glade under stone arches into a pool below.

In Chinese landscapes, water and mountains predominated — water, as the *yin*, or soft female; rocky promontories, as the *yang*, or strong male presence. Ancient Chinese stroll gardens featured winding trails that moved from one carefully staged garden vignette — perhaps a waterfall or viewing platform overlooking a stream or tranquil pool — to another.

Water was also a vital component of Japanese landscape design. Even in gardens without a source of water, pebbles formed streams, and sand or gravel was carefully raked until its ridges resembled waves. Design guides for building waterfalls, dating from the 12th century, are still in use today, with styles such as heaven-falling (water from a high source), thread-falling (thin rivulets of water) and right-and-left falling (divided).

Not only was water itself integral to the Japanese landscape, the method of spanning it was also important. Stepping stones and arched moon bridges (which reflected in still water as perfect circles) were popular, as well as *yatsubashi*, zigzag bridges designed to deter evil spirits who were thought to be able to move only in straight lines.

Many modern Japanese gardens feature a *tsukabai*, or stone basin, used in temple gardens for handwashing before the tea ceremony.

CHAPTER TWO

WATER
in your
GARDEN

*A*t its best,
a pond or pool adds a pleasing
dimension to any garden. Depending
on its size, it may serve as a strong
focal point for the garden or
become the dominant element within the
landscape. It can also alter a site
optically, creating the illusion of more
space than actually exists.

CHOOSING A LOCATION
for a POOL OR POND

The primary reason for creating a water feature is aesthetic, so it makes sense to put a pool or pond where it enhances the landscape you have (or plan to have), and where you can see it easily from the house. You should also consider the particular pleasure you wish to derive from water in your garden.

If you'd like to enjoy the cooling effect of water close at hand, you might consider incorporating a water feature in a deck, terrace or patio. Or you might use the mysterious sound of water around a corner or at the end of a path as an irresistible destination in the garden, enticing visitors and drawing them closer.

If you want to create a natural pond that will attract a rich variety of wildlife, you'll need to situate it far enough away from the house to encourage visits. Most animals and birds are too wary of humans to approach a pond that's too close to the house.

But there's no design rule that says you must hide your water feature in the back yard. Why not put it right beside the entrance to your front door? A sophisticated

Incorporating a pond in a patio (left) or allowing it to flow like a lake under a deck (right) lets garden visitors enjoy the cooling effect of water close at hand.

shallow reflecting pool will distinguish your home from others and give it street appeal.

If you have children, you'll want to keep your pond in clear view. And if you want a pond deeper than two feet or so, and you live in a city that has by-laws governing swimming pool depths, you may have to fence your property and install padlocks on the gate. (See Safety Considerations with a Pond, p. 44.)

SUN *or* SHADE?

Since a pond should convey a sense of belonging in the garden, rather than being an isolated element, try to find a spot where it can be well integrated into the plantings around it.

Is the proposed site in sun or shade? Most flowering pond plants require considerable sun to perform well. Hardy and tropical water lilies (*Nymphaea* spp.) need six hours of sun daily, and the bewitchingly beautiful sacred lotus (*Nelumbo nucifera*) won't even consider unfurling its exotic chalices without soaking up several weeks of hot, sunny weather which has warmed water temperatures to a simmering 22°C (75°F).

In order to maximize sunshine for flowering aquatics, the pond should be located where tall trees and shrubs likely to cast shade during the hottest part of the day are to the north. It should also be protected from winds that can rough up the water surface and keep water lilies from flowering (they prefer still water to bloom).

But a shady property doesn't spell the end of water-gardening dreams. Yellow pond lily (*Nuphar advena*) is a native water lily relative that thrives in fairly shady ponds, producing modest tulip-like blooms and masses of foliage. Bog arum (*Calla pallustris*), marsh marigold (*Caltha palustris*), yellow flag iris (*I. pseudacorus*) and sweet flag (*Acorus calamus*) are marginal aquatic plants that also tolerate shade. Some lovely effects are possible using moisture- and shade-loving ferns and hostas, combined with Japanese primrose, Japanese iris, globeflower, astilbe and the bold architectural forms of rodgersia, ligularia and ornamental rhubarb. (For more on moisture-loving plants, see p. 65.) And shade has one major advantage — algae, which thrive in sunlight, are much less bothersome in a shady pond.

OTHER SITE CONSIDERATIONS

❧ Are there large deciduous trees nearby with surface roots that will make pond excavation a difficult or impossible task? Will their fallen leaves foul the water in autumn? Decomposing leaves can have a detrimental effect on fish health, particularly in winter when they release lethal methane gas as they break down.

❧ Certain types of trees and plants should be avoided near fish ponds. Pine needles and oak and maple leaves release tannic acid which, in heavy concentrations, can be toxic to fish; laburnum flowers and seeds are also poisonous.

❧ What about bedrock? Underground utility cables? Plumbing pipes? Digging a pond is difficult enough without unforeseen obstacles making things tougher.

❧ Topography is important, too. Do you have a sloping property, or a flat, featureless site? The bottom of a sharp slope is not always the best place for a small pond because it will receive run-off which can muddy the water or lift the liner. If you decide on a pond here, you may need to build it so that the back side of the pond is embedded in the slope, with the front raised above-ground. Run-off routes, gravel drainage sumps or plastic weeping tiles may also need to be installed so the pond isn't flooded by rain and melting snow. The advantage of a sloping property is that it's the perfect place for a waterfall.

A grounded electrical outlet in the garden permits the use of pump-dependent water ornaments, such as these spouting frogs.

❧ Is there a tap close enough to the site so you can easily fill and replenish the pond when necessary? Is there an electrical outlet close at hand to supply power for lighting or for a recirculating pump for a fountain or waterfall? If not, is it possible to run conduit containing the appropriate wiring underground from your house to the site?

FORMAL POOL *or* NATURAL-LOOKING POOL?

Once you've decided where you'd like to situate a pond or pool, the next consideration is one of design. Of all the variables governing the creation of garden ponds and pools, the aesthetic ones are often the most difficult to achieve. Before you take shovel to hand, consider how water will fit into the existing landscape.

Is it appropriate to the garden? Is the style sympathetic to the architecture of the house? Is it an integral part of the property or a watery afterthought? In the final analysis, aesthetic considerations are as important as good workmanship.

Take a look at the architecture of your home and the style of your garden.

❦ Do you have a formal Georgian or Tudor-style house
with a wrought-iron fence, straight brick walkways and a
manicured landscape of clipped hedges and tidy rose
beds? An informal pond with sloping rocky banks,
bulrushes and tadpoles would be jarringly out of place
here. Instead, the setting suggests the symmetry and
perfect geometry of a formal pool. It could be square,
rectangular, oval or circular; in-ground or above-ground;
lined with flexible pond liner or fashioned from granite,
limestone, brick or cement. It might have a central
fountain with water jets, feature a classic piece of statuary,
or have stone-coped edges adorned with formal planters
filled with flowers and trailing ivy.

❦ A more contemporary house and a garden with
informal plantings, on the other hand, lends itself to a
naturalistic pond, which can be made to look as if it's
always been there. If a wooden deck is already in place,
additional decking can be extended over one or more
edges of the pond to suggest a lakeside cottage dock. If
the property borders on a meadow or woodland where a
stream or bog garden can be contrived, so much the better.

❦ On a brand-new property with few features and
plantings, where the garden is being created from scratch,
a naturalistic pond needs sensitive treatment with
perennials, ornamental grasses, shrubs and trees that will
grow quickly and be entirely appropriate to a waterside
setting. Here, nature's own ponds can be used as a design
guide. The advantage with a new garden, of course, is that
the water feature can be the focus around which the rest of
the garden is planned.

Without careful attention to the garden's theme,
however, a pond or pool — even if it's finished with
edging and plants that are in perfect harmony with its
own style — can be inappropriate to the landscape. As
tempting as it might be to introduce a Japanese-style
pond, complete with river rock, koi, bamboo spout, water
iris and stone lantern, in a traditional English border-style
garden, the Japanese touch will always be the garden
equivalent of a mixed metaphor.

WHAT ABOUT SIZE?

The ideal size for a naturalistic pond or formal pool is
one that's in scale with the house and the property itself.

❦ A country property with substantial acreage, particularly
one with clay soil and naturally occurring springs, can

A pond may be grandly formal (left), corresponding in style and size to an equally formal home and landscape — or it may nestle like a jewel in the tiniest shady nook.

sustain a pond big enough for a canoe and swimming raft.

❧ Even a small property can generally accommodate a larger water feature than you might think, particularly if the water can be made to disappear like a lake under cedar decking or a stone terrace, or to meander around and through planted garden peninsulas.

❧ Size, of course, is relative. A small, watery oasis tucked like a jewel in a corner of a big city garden will be a delight, but a tiny pond installed in a vast putting-green lawn will look like a comic puddle.

❧ A narrow lot is ideal for a formal reflecting pool, rectangular in shape, contemplative in mood, overhung by lush plantings mirrored in the water's surface. If a rugged, natural look is more in keeping with the property, you might consider a narrow watercourse reminiscent of a windswept northern river, defined by rocky shores and laid on a gentle grade to keep the water moving.

❧ It's generally better for a pond to be too big than too small, since crowded conditions can soon tip the ecological balance (see A Short Course in Pond Ecology, p. 20.) The water in a small, shallow pool also heats up too quickly, jeopardizing fish. Once installed and stocked, a large pond isn't much more difficult to maintain than a smaller one.

❧ But if yours is a truly tiny property with a truly tiny garden, a pond can be as simple as a washtub sunk into the earth and planted with a single pygmy water lily, its edges disguised with trailing plants, its "shore" graced with a diminutive shrub.

It's the quality, not the quantity, of water in a garden that's important.

AND SHAPE?

❧ A formal pool generally has a geometric shape — round, oval, rectangular, square, L-shape — and often mirrors the shape of nearby planting beds or walkways. It might be sunk into a formal lawn or paved terrace, or constructed partially or entirely above-ground.

❧ A natural pond has a curvilinear form, often interpreted as a crescent or kidney shape, and should mimic the random flowing shapes of nature's own ponds. Since a pond, by definition, is a natural depression filled with still water, the ideal location is in-ground with the water surface at the same level as the surrounding garden.

CHAPTER THREE

A SHORT COURSE *in* POND ECOLOGY

*N*ature has perfected a system of checks and balances for keeping pond life — fish, animals, plants, nutrients, waste and algae — in harmony. The successful creation and maintenance of a pond depend on how well the gardener understands and imitates this ecosystem.

THE ECOSYSTEM
of a POND

To enjoy pond gardening to its fullest and to maintain a healthy, balanced environment in and around the water, the wise gardener learns what each component of the ecosystem contributes to the mix, or bio-load; when and how to correct imbalances that might occur; and when to be patient and wait for nature to sort problems out. This is referred to as eco-balance.

Sunlight

All green plants need the sun's energy to fuel the process of photosynthesis. Chlorophyll and other light-capturing pigments in a leaf absorb and use sunlight to photolyze, or split, the water molecules the leaf receives from the plant roots into hydrogen atoms and molecular oxygen (O_2). At the same time, atmospheric carbon dioxide (CO_2) is absorbed through the pores, or stomata, in the leaf surfaces.

❧ During photosynthesis, the hydrogen and the carbon dioxide interact to make complex carbohydrates and simple sugars which are then used as food and building blocks by the plant. Oxygen essential to human survival is released into the atmosphere as a waste product of photosynthesis, which is why green leafy trees are often referred to as the earth's lungs.

❧ In a pond, photosynthesis in submerged oxygenating plants releases oxygen into the water during the day. At night, when the plants absorb oxygen to oxidize or metabolize plant sugars (called aerobic cellular respiration), carbon dioxide is released into the water. Submerged aquatic plants that don't have leaf stomata absorb gases and water over their entire surface. Some floating plants have stomata on the upper surface of their leaves.

❧ As well as providing the radiant energy for photosynthesis, the sun also stimulates flowering in all plants, including aquatics such as water lilies. But too much sun in a shallow pond can raise the water temperature to a level harmful to fish. The sun also promotes the growth of undesirable green algae, especially in spring. Therefore, it's usually recommended that 60 to 70 percent of a pond's surface be shaded by floating aquatic plants.

❧ Sunlight is also vital to the health of the oxygenating plants, which do their part in controlling algae by competing for the nutrients algae need to thrive.

Water

❧ Most municipal tap water contains chlorine, which kills bacteria that can be toxic to humans. But chlorine can also burn fish gills and harm aquatic plants. A volatile gas, chlorine dissipates into the atmosphere from standing water within 24 hours. However, to stabilize chlorine and make its effects long lasting, some water treatment plants also add ammonia to create chloramines. Ammonia at any level in a pond can be toxic to fish. Water containing chloramines should be treated with a chemical dechlorinator (e.g. *Aqua-Safe, Water Prep Plus*).

❧ When topping up a pond with tap water, spray the water into the pond with a hose nozzle to help aerate it. A submersible pump with a fountain jet or outlet that lifts water to the air also introduces oxygen, benefiting fish respiration and enabling microscopic nitrifying bacteria (see Fish, p. 25) to do their work. Try not to add more tap water than 5 to 10 percent of the pond's volume per week. Again, if a large fish population is present, use a dechlorinating product. If a large quantity of tap water needs to be added (for example, after repairing a leak), remove fish temporarily to an alternative holding tank containing reserved pond water.

❦ Rainwater, of course, offers a safe way of topping up a pond, and can be collected easily by placing a rain barrel under your roof's downpipe. Some cities now offer free programs to disconnect downpipes and hook up rain barrels.

❦ Water hardness is governed by the amount of calcium carbonate and magnesium present, and is measured on a scale from 1-30 dH (degree of hardness), with 1 degree equalling 17.1 ppm (parts per million) and 30 degrees equalling 535 ppm. Soft water is 4-8 dH, medium-hard is 8-17 dH and hard is 17-30 dH. Fish thrive at 3-12 dH (50-200 ppm) but a hardness up to 17 dH or slightly more is acceptable. Serious problems can arise with very soft water combined with very alkaline (high pH) conditions.

❦ Water pH is the degree of acidity or alkalinity and is measured on a scale of 1-14, with a reading of 7 being neutral. Acid conditions give a reading of lower than 7; alkaline is higher than 7. For fish, the ideal pH range is 6-8.5. Higher pH, or more alkaline conditions — which can be caused by leaching of calcium carbonate into a poorly sealed concrete pool or from concrete blocks — can cause fish stress, infections and death.

❦ Kits for testing pond water are available at water-garden suppliers.

Fish

Goldfish, koi and other ornamental fish bring a flash of color and a sense of play to a naturalistic pond. They're entertaining to watch and do their part in maintaining a pleasant garden environment by devouring mosquito larvae, which can be an annoying problem around still ponds. Fish also eat algae and may dine on the roots of some pond plants.

❦ But fish can upset the biological balance in a pond. Fish excreta is high in toxic ammonia and because fish won't survive in waste-polluted water, some means of reducing the ammonia level is needed. Ammonia is also food for algae. To curb ammonia, thus safeguarding fish and reducing algae, it's vital that a fish pond has sufficient levels of nitrifying bacteria to control algae growth.

❦ A certain level of nitrifying bacteria occurs in pond water naturally, but in a small, highly stocked fish pond where high levels of ammonia occur, it may be necessary to seed the pond with a beneficial bacteria additive, such as *Bacta-Pur Klear*. Large fish ponds require biological filtration.

❦ Because fish breathe by extracting oxygen from water drawn in through their gills, pond water must contain adequate oxygen. Oxygen is available from the air at the pond's surface but it's also supplied by submerged oxygenating plants (e.g., elodea, hornwort) and, to a lesser extent, by fountains or waterfalls which introduce oxygen by aerating the water.

❦ But even in a pond with a waterfall or fountain left operating during the night, fish are sometimes seen at the surface in the morning gasping for air. This happens because oxygen is depleted and high levels of carbon dioxide are produced — by the fish as they exhale and by the normal cellular respiration of plants during the night. In hot weather, particularly if there aren't enough floating plants (60 to 70 percent of the pond's surface) to keep the water shaded and cool, the water temperature will rise and oxygen will evaporate more quickly. At the same time, too many floating plants can prevent adequate absorption of oxygen through the water surface. To combat low oxygen levels, an air pump similar to an aquarium pump may be needed. Large fish ponds may require an air compressor.

Fish in a pond are both beautiful to look at and beneficial. By consuming mosquito larvae, they help maintain a pleasant garden environment.

❧ Fish, especially koi, can muddy the water by rooting in the pots of marginal aquatic plants. Plants should be mulched with a layer of pea gravel or sand to prevent this.

❧ In a pond with lots of plants and a small number of goldfish, fish food is not required — bugs, mosquito larvae, algae and some aquatic plants provide an ample diet. But if koi or a large number of smaller fish live in the pond, supplemental feedings are required. Because uneaten fish food can break down into ammonia and upset the water's balance, feed fish only what they can consume in 2 to 3 minutes.

❧ To ensure fish stay healthy, it's important to keep their population at a safe level. Fish not only grow but spawn, especially if they're fed regularly; unfed goldfish usually consume their own eggs. Taking mature fish size into account, the standard rule in stocking a new pond is no more than 1 inch of fish per 2 square feet of surface area. Excess fish should be given away.

❧ In a highly stocked fish pond, levels of ammonia, nitrite and nitrate should be measured regularly with a pond-testing kit (see p. 87).

Biofilters, Mechanical Filters *and* Ammonia Neutralizers

If you want a large number of fish, especially koi, you'll likely need a biological filtration system, or biofilter, that pumps pond water slowly through a special filtration medium — gravel, batting, cloth, sponge — which has been colonized by nitrifying bacteria. These bacteria normally occur in pond water but, to be truly effective in clearing waste, they should be concentrated in large numbers. In the filter media, they are safe from preying fish and well-supplied with oxygen from the pumped water.

❧ Biofilters range in size from small models for 50- to 150-gallon ponds to large multi-arm models swathed in filter cloth for ponds of 1,500 to 1,800 gallons in size. External biological filters that move water past brushes and through various chambers are available for even larger koi ponds. Bubble bead filters handle up to 15,000 gallons.

❧ To be effective, a biofilter must operate full-time, since shutting it down for more than a few hours can kill the nitrifying bacteria. The pump should allow the entire pond to recirculate slowly every 2 hours (for example, a 1,000-gallon pond should have a pump that recirculates 500 gallons per hour).

❧ Because many biofilters are also mechanical filters (the reverse, however, is not true), they must be cleaned during the summer season, when water flow has slowed by about 25 percent. This should be done as quickly as

Oxygenators

Oxygenating plants such as hornwort (*Ceratophyllum demersum*), sagittaria (*S. subulata*), Canadian pondweed (*Elodea canadensis*) and ribbon grass (*Vallisneria americana*) absorb nitrates that also stimulate growth of undesirable algae. They simultaneously release oxygen into the pond water, which can be seen as bubbles rising to the surface on a sunny day. The oxygen aids fish respiration and provides the aerobic conditions required for nitrifying bacteria to do their work.

Depending on their growth habit, oxygenators are planted in pots or tossed into the water as cuttings. Because even rooted oxygenators absorb nutrients through their foliage, it is not necessary to plant them in soil — pea gravel is adequate. The recommended stocking level is one bunch of cuttings per 2 to 3 square feet of pond surface. To reduce the number of in-pond containers, some experts recommend planting rooted oxygenators in the same pots as water lilies.

If a well-established algae bloom is present when you're adding oxygenators to your pond in spring, it may be necessary to place the potted ones nearer the sunny surface. (Oxygenating plants also provide an excellent habitat for spawning fish and a protective cover for fish fry.)

perfectly clear view of pots, pumps, cables and all the artifice that a pond owner may wish to hide.

Pond water should **not** be changed to clear up an algae bloom. Tap water contains dissolved minerals — in other words, algae food — and starts the entire cycle all over again. Chemical algicides such as potassium permanganate and copper sulphate are not recommended because they can injure snails and slow the growth of aquatic plants.

Operators of fish-free formal ponds at some botanic gardens — for example, Longwood Gardens in Pennsylvania — use an aquatic dye such as *Deep Water Shade* to combat algae. The dye prevents the specific light waves used by algae from fueling photosynthesis, ultimately starving the algae, but it does not affect the health of water lilies. The water appears blue-green in color, but it's clear rather than murky.

Snails *and* Tadpoles

Ramshorn snails (*Planorbis corneus*) and trapdoor snails (*Viviparis malleatus*) are beneficial scavengers in a pond, eating algae as well as decaying plant material and excess fish food. Snails should be added at the rate of one per square foot of pond surface. Because trapdoor snails bear their young live, unlike the ramshorn, which deposits its eggs in jellied masses under lily leaves, many gardeners prefer the trapdoors. Frog tadpoles also feed on algae and excess nutrients.

Landscaping *the* Pond

*Positioning plants, such as the dwarf hemlocks (above)
or the hosta (below), right at the water's edge creates a beautiful reflection while
integrating the pond into the surrounding garden.*

To make an attractive transition from the pond to the surrounding landscape, the gardener can choose from a huge palette of flowering and foliage perennials, ornamental grasses, conifers, flowering shrubs and trees. Restraint is key; try to avoid planting one of everything. The reflective quality of still water has the strongest impact when brilliantly colored plants are massed in drifts, or when bold foliage forms and architectural shapes are allowed to dominate rather than compete with others.

To suggest a natural setting for your pond, try to obscure the artificial boundaries and features in your garden. Disguise fences and garage walls with evergreen hedges (cedar, laurel, yew, hemlock) and lush vines (trumpet vine, euonymus, Virginia creeper).

Avoid the fish-pond-in-the-lawn syndrome by setting the pond in its own landscape to separate it from the manicured lawn. And try not to resort to bedding plants like petunias, impatiens or snapdragons near the pond — save those for the flower beds.

If your pond has an Oriental theme, carry it through to the landscape. Choose elegant, understated plantings that convey a feeling of tranquility. Weeping trees have a special affinity to Oriental gardens, and look charming with branches draped over still water. Consider weeping cultivars of Japanese cherry, katsura, ginkgo, white pine, crab apple and Japanese maple.

MAKING *a* WATERFALL

Waterfalls are often used in large gardens to exploit natural level changes or as part of a hillside rock garden. But any garden can incorporate a small waterfall as a lively addition to a naturalistic pond, and even the smallest garden is enhanced by the sound of water trickling over a cairn of rocks. Ultra-modern architectural styles or commercial landscapes may suggest a less nature-based approach — a water wall, for example, where water flows down the face of a granite or marble slab in perfectly symmetrical fashion, in tune with the other built features.

Apart from their aesthetic role, waterfalls aerate and improve the ecological quality of pond water. In small waterfalls, a lower pond contains the submersible pump, which forces the water via flexible reinforced tubing back to the top. A longer waterfall requiring a large volume of water may need a powerful external pump. A waterfall descending through more than one pool might require a submersible pump for each pool.

You can build a waterfall from scratch to suit the contours of your garden (right), or you can save time and labor by incorporating a prefabricated stone waterfall unit (below), available in a variety of styles from water-garden suppliers.

MAKING *a* PEBBLE BEACH

In the stream-like shallow pond at left, pebbles and smooth rocks were placed on top of the pond liner to form the gently sloped shores and floor. Alternatively, a simple pebble beach can be fashioned on a wider underwater shelf in the pond, as illustrated below.

Rather than having straight walls around the entire pond, consider turning one side into a gently sloped pebble or gravel beach.

A beach encourages wildlife to visit the pond. It also integrates the pond into the garden, provides an overflow area for pond water during heavy rains and allows toads and frogs to leave the water once they've evolved from the tadpole stage.

❦ As you dig the pond, make a shelf — 2 feet (60 cm) wide and as long as you want the beach to be — approximately 6 inches (15 cm) below the pond rim. At the front edge, lay a curb of stones or bricks on end, covering it with extra underlay to avoid puncturing the liner.

❦ When it's time to put the underlay and liner in place, spread them over the curb and the shelf, leaving at least a foot of overhang at the pond rim.

❦ Pour pea gravel or smooth stones onto the shelf to create a gentle slope toward the pond bank. Lift the liner at the top and mound earth underneath to create a slightly higher grade than the pond rim. This prevents erosion of the beach by rain.

❦ Soil can then be placed on the gravel above the waterline, and mulch placed over the liner edge. Pea gravel is a good planting medium for marginals such as arrowhead, cardinal flower and zebra rush. Smooth river rocks and boulders can be placed here and there on the pea gravel, as they might appear on a northern shore.

WHAT *about* *a* BOG GARDEN?

What is a bog? When it comes to separating one damp place from another, confused gardeners often tend to be less than specific. But nature is never vague in differentiating wetland habitats.

BOGS

A bog is a nutrient-poor, acidic wetland that derives its water from rainfall. The surface layer is sphagnum moss (hence the term "peat bog") and is often quite dry and spongy.

❧ True bog plants are acid-loving and include native species such as highbush blueberry (*Vaccinium corymbosum*), Labrador tea (*Ledum groenlandicum*), bog laurel (*Kalmia polifolia*) and cranberry (*Vaccinium oxycoccum*). Trees might include tamarack, black spruce (*Picea mariana*) and swamp birch (*Betula pumila*).

❧ Many bog plants are evergreen to permit year-round photosynthesis; some, like pitcher plant (*Sarracenia purpurea*), rely on insects, rather than soil, for their nutrients.

A bog garden planted with delicate pink astilbe and stately Japanese iris makes a lovely counterpoint to this quiet pond.

Although there is no pond in this damp ravine, Japanese iris, yellow loosestrife and red astilbe thrive in the rich, marshy soil.

FENS

A fen receives its water from precipitation and from groundwater discharge such as that from an underground spring. A natural spring-fed country pond is, in scientific terms, a fen.

MARSHES

A marsh is a nutrient-rich wetland (freshwater or saltwater) that relies on precipitation and surface runoff from streams, rivers, ponds and lakes. Marshes generally have some standing water on a permanent basis,

but marsh plants are those adapted to seasonal changes in moisture levels — high in spring and fall and lower in summer.

❧ Common marsh plants include horsetail, cattail, arrowhead, spike rush, bulrush, bog arum, sweet flag, blue flag and great blue lobelia.

SWAMPS

There are two kinds — shrub swamps and tree swamps. A swamp receives its water and nutrients via overland flows from a river or nearby lake, or from ground sources such as springs. It might have

standing water most of the year, or become relatively dry in summer.

❧ Common plants found in swamps include red osier dogwood, willow, buttonbush, white cedar, tamarack, balsam fir, red maple, silver maple and black ash.

So, although we might refer to a damp garden as a "bog garden," in reality it is a freshwater marsh garden filled with native or non-native plants that are indigenous to wet meadows or to the marshy soil beside rivers, lakes and streams. And this is what you should be aiming for when you create a bog garden beside your pond.

Making *a* Bog Garden

A bog garden can be made adjacent to a pond to utilize the overflow caused by rain, or simply to soften the pond's edges, enhancing it with the type of landscape that might naturally occur beside a body of water. A bog garden can also be built independently of a pond — to exploit an area with poor drainage, or contrived artificially for the sole purpose of growing moisture-loving plants.

❦ Dig the area out to between 16 and 18 inches (40 to 45 cm) deep, removing the sod and topsoil to a tarp or plastic sheet, and the subsoil to the compost or to a waterfall construction, if that is part of the pond project. If the bog excavation is root-filled or very rocky, it may be advisable to line the excavation with geotextile before laying down a sheet of 30- to 40-mil PVC or 45-mil EPDM pond liner. (You can also use a rigid fiberglass pond shell, its bottom punctured for drainage, as a small bog garden.)

❦ If you're building the bog garden in conjunction with a pond, you may wish to extend the liner directly from the pond into the bog excavation. Keep the pond edging higher than the bog (use a boulder or concrete block underneath it, if necessary) to prevent backflow of the bog soil into the pond. Use a pitchfork to poke holes every 6 inches or so in the liner bottom.

❦ Fill the lined excavation with the sod, turned upside down, followed by the reserved topsoil amended in a 1:1 ratio with humus, to a depth of between 1 and 2 inches (2.5 to 5 cm) from the original soil level. Compost and leaf mold make good humus, but the easiest and cheapest humus for a bog garden is peat moss, thoroughly moistened with warm water. Peat moss is acidic, but most moisture-loving plants tend to like acid soils.

❦ If the soil remains very mucky, you may need to incorporate some sand or to poke a few more holes in the liner bottom. If the soil is very dry, you will need to water the garden on a frequent basis or install a simple drip irrigation system or a soaker hose. Another possible remedy for a bog garden that dries too quickly is to incorporate water-retaining polymer crystals in the soil. The garden should also be well mulched to prevent evaporation in periods of drought.

❦ Plant the bog garden with your favorite moisture-loving plants (see list, p. 65). Very wet areas in a bog garden can be planted with hardy emergent or marginal pond plants recommended for planting at water level (see Plants for Ponds, p. 77).

Japanese primroses thrive in the damp soil of a pond (below).

The first hardy water lily hybrids were developed by the French breeder, Marliac, in the late 19th century; many of his crosses continue to be popular today. One of the foremost tropical hybridizers was George Pring of Missouri, and many popular tropicals bear his patent name.

All water lilies need full sun (6 hours) and warm water for maximum flower production. Hardy lilies are planted from late April to June, when the water temperature has reached 15°C (60°F). Colder water may stunt growth. Tropicals need a starting temperature of 20°C (70°F) and are planted in May or June, depending on climate zone. But tropicals will continue flowering into early autumn, depending on water temperatures, well after hardy lilies have gone dormant.

Hardy and tropical water lilies are heavy feeders, requiring rich heavy soil. Supplemental fertilizer can take the form of special aquatic organic fertilizer, fertilizer tablets or slow-release fertilizer briquettes especially formulated for aquatic plants and used only once per season. Hardy water lilies must be divided every 1 to 3 years to retain their vigor.

Water lilies make excellent cut flowers. Conditioned well, they can last 4 to 5 days; leave the cut flowers floating in the sun for 30 minutes, then use a dab of wax or nail polish on the base of each petal to prevent it from closing.

pea gravel to a depth of at least 1 inch (2.5 cm). The gravel holds the soil in the basket, protects the crown and prevents soil from washing over it.

STEP 5

❧ Carefully lower the basket into the pond. To achieve the right height, set containers on bricks or pavers on the bottom of the pond.
❧ The type of water lily will dictate the depth of planting: from 2 to

should remain just above the surface — soil in the crown can prevent good growth. Water again, allowing the soil to settle; check to be sure the crown is still at the right level.
❧ If the soil is rich, fertilizing at planting time is not essential. If desired, push 3 fertilizer tablets, such as *Sera* or *Pondtabbs*, a couple of inches (5 cm) into the soil.

STEP 4

❧ When the second watering has completely settled and the position of the crown has been checked and adjusted, cover the soil surface with

4 inches (5 to 10 cm) of water above the crown for the tropical blue-flowered *Nymphaea colorata*, to 3 feet (1 m) or more for the hardy white cultivar, 'Gladstone'. Because water near the surface of the pond is warmer than deep water, tropical hybrids are generally planted with 4 inches (10 cm) of water over the crown for the first month, then lowered to between 6 and 8 inches (15 to 20 cm). For correct planting depth for individual lilies, check with your water-garden supplier.

Hardy water lilies are not bothered by many pests but can be susceptible to a fungal disease called crown rot, in which the rhizome becomes mushy, foliage is sparsely produced and turns yellow soon after unfolding, and flower buds rot and fall before opening. Since crown rot is difficult to combat and is highly contagious, it's best to buy your hardy lilies from a reputable dealer, preferably one who grows his or her own nursery stock.

Insect pests include water lily beetles and plum aphid. Use a hose to wash them off the leaves into the pond, where they make a tasty meal for fish.

Overwintering Water Lilies

HARDY VARIETIES

❧ Hardy water lilies may be overwintered in their containers in the pond, provided the roots do not freeze solid. If the pond has a deep zone where water does not freeze — from 2.5 to 6 feet (0.8 to 2 m), depending on the frost line in your area — the container should be moved there.

❧ Alternatively, lilies can be lifted in their containers before freeze-up and, after their foliage has been removed, they can be stored in a cool cellar or garage (5 to 10°C/40 to 50°F) for the winter. Do not let rhizomes dry out. In spring, new growth will appear and lilies can be put back in the pond, or removed from the pot and divided, if tubers have become crowded.

TROPICAL VARIETIES

❧ Tropicals are usually treated as (rather expensive) annuals. Although overwintering can be attempted in the same way that hardy lilies are treated, the outcome is not guaranteed.

❧ Alternatively, you can wait until the pond water has cooled to 10°C (50°F), then bring the lily in its container into a cool basement or garage. Remove the plant from the pot and rinse off the dirt, then allow it to air-dry for 2 to 3 days before cutting off the leaves and stems.

❧ Separate the tubers (new ones may have formed) and place them in lukewarm water for 24 hours. Check the condition of the submerged tubers — those that sank can be saved, while the others should be discarded.

❧ Air-dry the retained tubers in a cool room for a few days, then place them in the middle of cool, damp (not wet) sand in a plastic bag. Store the closed bag at 13°C (55°F) until four weeks before the last frost date in your area.

❧ If the tubers have sprouted, place each in a 5-inch (12 cm) pot, barely covering it with heavy topsoil, then with a layer of pebbles. If not, place them in water on a sunny windowsill to sprout.

❧ Place pots with sprouted tubers in a tub or fish tank and cover with water heated to between 20 and 22°C (70 to 74°F). Use an aquarium heater to heat the water. When new growth begins, the tubers should be moved to a well-lit area, or fluorescent lights can be set up over the tank.

❧ When the pond has warmed to 20°C (70°F), the tubers can be transplanted in fresh soil in containers and returned to their summer home.

Unless hardy water lilies can be moved to deep water where their rhizomes will not freeze in winter, they should be lifted in autumn and stored in a cool place indoors.

Hardy Water Lilies

With a small spread (4 to 5 square feet) and suitable for tubs or small ponds

PINK
- 'Pink Opal'
- 'Joanne Pring'

WHITE
- N. odorata pumila * (Zone 4)
- N. tetragona (Zone 3)
- 'Candida'

YELLOW
- 'Pygmaea Helvola' (very tiny)

CHANGEABLE
- 'Aurora'
- 'Graziella'
- 'Indiana'
- 'Little Sue'
- 'Paul Harriot'

With a medium-large spread (6 to 10 square feet)

PINK
- 'Arc en Ciel' *
- 'Fabiola'
- 'Gloire de temple sur Lot'
- 'Hollandia'
- 'Marliac Carnea'
- 'Marliac Rose'
- 'Mary'
- 'Masaniello'
- 'Nigel'
- 'Norma Gedye'
- 'Pearl of the Pool' *
- 'Pink Pumpkin'
- 'Pink Sensation'
- 'Pink Sunrise'
- 'Rose Arey'
- 'Yuh Ling'

RED
- 'Burgundy Princess'
- 'Gloriosa'
- 'James Brydon'
- 'Laydekeri Fulgens' (or smaller)
- 'Liou' (or smaller)
- 'Mayla'
- 'Red Spider'

WHITE
- 'Gonnere'
- 'Hal Miller'
- 'Hermine'
- 'Marliac White'
- 'Mme. Julien Chifflot'
- 'Virginalis'

YELLOW
- 'Charlene Strawn'
- 'Chromatella'
- 'Moorei'
- 'Lemon Chiffon'

CHANGEABLE
- 'Sioux'

With a large spread (10 to 12 square feet)

PINK
- 'Amabilis'
- 'Firecrest'

RED
- 'Attraction'
- 'Charles de Meurville'
- 'Escarboucle'
- 'Rembrandt'
- 'Sultan'

WHITE
- Nymphaea alba (Zone 6)
- Nymphaea odorata * (Zone 4)
- 'Gladstone'

YELLOW
- 'Sunrise'

CHANGEABLE
- 'Comanche'

Tropical Water Lilies

Day-blooming, with a small spread (3 to 4 square feet)

BLUE
- Nympahea colorata
- 'Dauben'

Day-blooming, with a medium-large spread (8 to 16 square feet)

PINK/RED
- 'Castelliflora'
- 'General Pershing'
- 'Jack Ward'
- 'Madame Ganna Walska'
- 'Pink Capensis'
- 'Pink Pearl'
- 'Pink Platter'

WHITE
- 'Crystal'
- 'Marion Strawn' (or smaller)

BLUE/PURPLE/VIOLET
- 'August Koch'
- 'Blue Star' (or smaller)
- 'Blue Triumph Hybrid'
- 'Director Moore'
- 'Electra'
- 'King of the Blues'
- 'Marmota'
- 'Mrs. Martin Randig'
- 'Midnight'
- 'Nora'
- 'Panama Pacific'
- 'Tina'

YELLOW
- 'St. Louis Gold' (or smaller)

APRICOT
- 'Albert Greenberg'
- 'Golden West'

GREEN
- 'Green Smoke'

Day-blooming, with a large spread (16 to 25 square feet)

PINK/RED
- 'Mrs. C.W. Ward'

WHITE
- 'Mrs. George H. Pring'
- 'White Delight'

BLUE/PURPLE/VIOLET
- 'Blue Beauty'
- 'William Stone'

YELLOW
- 'Yellow Dazzler'

Night-blooming, with a medium-large spread (8 to 16 square feet)

PINK/RED
- 'Emily Grant Hutchings'
- 'Red Cup'
- 'Red Flare'
- 'Sturtevanti'
- 'Texas Shell Pink'

WHITE
- 'Wood's White Night'

Night-blooming, with a large spread (16 to 25 square feet)

PINK/RED
- 'Mrs. George C. Hitchcock'
- 'Maroon Beauty'
- 'Rubra'

WHITE
- 'Missouri'
- 'Sir Galahad'

* Nymphaea odorata *hybrids — plant rhizomes horizontally*

PLANTS FOR PONDS *and* POOLS

Lotuses (*Nelumbo* spp.)

SACRED LOTUS
(*Nelumbo nucifera*)

❧ Native to the Orient, this sacred flower of the Hindu religion has been in cultivation for at least 2,500 years. Leaves can reach between 1 and 2 feet (30 to 60 cm) in length and often rise on strong stems more than 4 feet (1.3 m) above the water. Flowers are often fragrant, large (to 12 inches/30 cm), either white or pink (*N. nucifera speciosum*) and look like huge roses. They develop distinctive seedheads which look like shower nozzles and are often used in dried arrangements. Seed is viable for hundreds of years.

❧ Plant banana-shape tubers horizontally 2 inches (5 cm) deep in rich soil in a very large planting container, taking care not to damage the fragile growing tip which should just poke out of the soil. Start under 4 to 6 inches (10 to 15 cm) of water at first, lowering to 12 inches (30 cm) as plants develop. Slow to establish, only leaves may develop the first year.

❧ Sacred lotus and its cultivars require many weeks of warm, sunny weather to flower. Cultivars can be winter-hardy to Zone 6, especially if planted in an earth-bottom pond or in containers in water deep enough so crown and tuber do not freeze. Winter care is the same as that of hardy water lilies.

Sacred Lotus (Nelumbo nucifera)

CULTIVARS

❧ 'CHAWAN BASU' — delicate, pink-edged white flowers. Prolific. Good for small ponds and tubs.

❧ 'MAGGIE BELLE SLOCUM' — magenta blooms with petals folded like quills. Adapts to ponds and small tubs.

❧ 'MOMO BATAN' — double dark rose flowers, a little like a peony on small plants. Suitable for a small pond or tub culture.

❧ 'MRS. PERRY SLOCUM' — huge flowers (often 12 inches/30 cm) that open deep pink, take on yellow tones the second day and turn creamy yellow-pink by the third.

❧ 'PERRY'S GIANT SUNBURST' — huge, elegant flowers of pale sulphur-yellow.

YELLOW AMERICAN LOTUS
(*Nelumbo lutea*)

❧ Native from southern Ontario into the southern United States. Large, round, blue-green leaves and 10-inch (25 cm) pale yellow flowers are both held high above the water. Hardier than sacred lotus and used in cross-breeding with that tender species. Needs rich soil and warm temperatures to flower. Zone 6.

POND LILIES
(*Nuphar* spp.)

❦ Pond lilies are best in very large, earth-bottom ponds. Their aggressive root systems make container planting difficult at best.

❦ YELLOW POND LILY (*Nuphar advena*) — very hardy North American native, with heart-shape leaves and small, yellow tulip-like flowers. Needs some sun to flower well. Zone 5.

❦ YELLOW WATER LILY (*Nuphar lutea*) — yellow buttercup-like flowers. Prefers deep (6 feet/2 m), somewhat acidic, often moving, water. Vigorous. Zone 5.

Oxygenating Plants

❦ CANADIAN PONDWEED, WATERWEED (*Elodea canadensis*) — hardy native North American, with branched stems and lacy whorled leaves. May be rooted in soil or pea gravel, or used as free-floating cuttings. Leaves are eaten by goldfish and used as habitat for fish fry. Excellent oxygenator but can be invasive in natural, clay-bottom ponds. Zone 4.

❦ HORNWORT (*Ceratophyllum demersum*) — very hardy native North American that grows entirely submerged, bearing branched stems with whorls of fine, bristle-like leaves. Tolerant of cold, deep water (to 30 feet/10 m), but also an excellent shallow-pond oxygenator and habitat for fish spawn and fry. Best and easiest oxygenator to use

because it doesn't require a pot — cuttings can simply be dropped into the water. Zone 5.

❦ RIBBON GRASS OR EEL GRASS (*Vallisneria americana*) — North American native, sometimes called wild celery, with light-green ribbon-shape leaves. Grows to 24 inches (60 cm). Popular food for ducks and waterfowl. Requires planting in soil; cuttings can be easily rooted. Tender.

Free-Floating Aquatic Plants

❦ DUCKWEED (*Lemna minor*) — a true aquatic fern, with small leaves and no flowers. It multiplies quickly to shade pond and control algae. Good fish food. Sometimes appears in ponds without being planted, since it is carried on the feathers of ducks. Invasive. Zone 5.

❦ FAIRY MOSS (*Azolla caroliniana*) — fuzzy floating carpet of tiny, fern-like plants. Green in summer, but turns crimson in cool weather. Frost-tender but might be overwintered indoors in a stock pan of pond soil and water.

❦ FROG'S BIT (*Hydrocharis morsus-ranae*) — small white flowers in spring and round floating leaves. Stolons spread horizontally, making tiny new plants at their ends. In natural ponds, new plants drop to the bottom in fall, then sprout the next spring and rise to the surface again. Invasive. Zone 5.

❦ WATER FERN OR WATER VELVET (*Salvinia rotundifolia*) — aquatic fern with small, hairy floating leaves that

appear dry, even after being submerged. Shade tolerant. Aggressive. Tender.

❦ WATER HYACINTH (*Eichornia crassipes major*) — very popular floating aquatic with spongy air-filled leaves and attractive purple

Water Hyacinth (Eichornia crassipes major)

flowers marked with yellow. Very long trailing roots provide spawning habitat for fish and deprive algae of nutrients. Used industrially to purify polluted water. Flowering is often sparse, which may be due to the roots being eaten by fish, so netting protector is advisable. Flowering also improves when roots anchor, rather than float unattached. Frost-tender but might overwinter in moist soil in a greenhouse or sunroom.

❦ WATER LETTUCE (*Pistia stratiotes*) — no flowers but attractive rosettes of blue-green leaves. Good plant for fish spawning and protection, and an excellent shade plant to control algae. Use netting protector to deter browsing koi. Tender, but may overwinter in a greenhouse or sunroom aquarium.

❧ WATER MEAL (*Wolffia* spp.) — very tiny aquatic fern that looks like surface algae. Smallest free-floater, fast to multiply, but easily scooped out. Tender.

❧ WATER POPPY (*Hydrocleyes nymphoides*) — a profusion of yellow poppy-like flowers held above glossy leaves. Excellent for small ponds and tubs. Tender.

Water Poppy (Hydrocleyes nymphoides)

Hardy Marginal (or Emergent) Aquatic Plants

Emergent or marginal plants are those that survive with roots or lower stems submerged in varying depths of water on a permanent basis. Those planted at water level may also thrive in the moist soil of a bog. (See Plants for Bog Gardens, p. 65.)

For Planting *at* Water Level

❧ ALLEGHENY MONKEY FLOWER (*Mimulus ringens*) — native from Nova Scotia to Manitoba. 1 to 2 feet (30 to 60 cm) high, with violet-blue flowers. Zone 4.

❧ ARROW ARUM (*Peltandra virginica*) — native plant bearing long, shiny, arrow-shape leaves and inconspicuous green flowers in May-June; may be followed by green berries. Grows to 3 feet (1 m). Zone 6.

❧ BOG ARUM (*Calla palustris*) — small calla-type bloom of white spathe surrounding a yellow spadix in spring which, if pollinated by pond snails, produces red berries. Needs quiet water. Grows 9 to 12 inches (22 to 30 cm) tall. Zone 5.

❧ CARDINAL FLOWER (*Lobelia cardinalis*) — beautiful native with deep red flowers on 3- to 4-foot (1 to 1.3 m) spikes. Attracts hummingbirds. Likes part shade and wet soil near streams. Adapts to deeper standing water. Lowering crown under water in fall might prevent death of plant in winter. Good bog plant. Zone 4.

Cardinal Flower (Lobelia cardinalis)

❧ GREAT BLUE LOBELIA (*L. siphilitica*) — this native blooms from August to September, with vivid blue-purple flower spikes on 2- to 3-foot (60 to 90 cm) stems. Tolerant of standing water. Best when divided every few years. Zone 6.

❧ HOUTTUYNIA (*H. cordata*) — sometimes called chameleon plant because of its striking green/red variegated foliage and white flowers. Also used as damp-border perennial. Grows 6 to 12 inches (15 to 30 cm) high. Invasive. Zone 6.

Marsh Marigold (Caltha palustris)

❧ MARSH MARIGOLD (*Caltha palustris*) — very adaptable native, with kidney-shape leaves and bright yellow buttercup-like flowers in early spring. Foliage sometimes disappears in summer and reappears in fall. Grows 9 to 15 inches (22 to 38 cm) tall. Beautiful paired with water forget-me-not. Double-flowered form is *C. palustris* 'Plena'. White form is *C. p.* 'Alba'. Zone 4.

❧ MICRO-MINIATURE CATTAIL (*Typha minima*) — better behaved than other cattails, this Japanese species grows 1 to 2 feet (30 to 60 cm) tall. Good for small ponds. Zone 6.

❧ SWAMP MILKWEED (*Asclepias incarnata*) — along with dry-land milkweeds, this native plant is the larval food for the monarch butterfly. Dull pink summer flower clusters. Grows 3 to 5 feet (90 to 150 cm) high. Good bog plant. Zone 4.

❧ VARIEGATED MANNA GRASS (*Glyceria aquatica* 'Variegata') — good foliage plant, with green, white and yellow striped leaves. Grows 18 to 24 inches (45 to 60 cm) tall. Zone 5.

❧ WATER FORGET-ME-NOT (*Myosotis palustris* or *M. scorpiodes*) — clambering stems and bright blue yellow-centered flowers, much like biennial forget-me-not, but blooms later and over a long period of time. Good in bogs. Zone 6.

Water Forget-Me-Not (Myosotis palustris)

For Planting 2 Inches (4 cm) Deep

❧ ARROWHEAD (*Sagittaria latifolia*) — this native has grass-like foliage when young, then develops typical arrowhead leaves. Tall spikes of delicate white flowers grow to 2 feet (60 cm). Good for protecting pond banks against erosion. Double arrowhead is *S. japonica* 'Flore Pleno', with beautiful double, white, carnation-like flowers. Zone 6.

Arrowhead (Sagittaria latifolia)

❧ BLUE WATER IRIS OR BLUE FLAG (*I. versicolor*) — native that blooms in May and June, with several blue-violet flowers on 18- to 24-inch (45 to 60 cm) stems. Zone 4.

❧ CATTAIL (*Typha latifolia*) — a common sight in marshes, ditches and pond margins where conditions range from wet soil to several feet of standing water. Velvety brown pokers

Cattail (Typha latifolia)

have separated male and female flower segments. Grows to height of between 6 and 9 feet (2 to 3 m). Creeping rhizomes are highly invasive — must be planted in containers. Zone 4.

❧ CORKSCREW RUSH (*Juncus effusus* 'Spiralis') — interesting spiral shape to the stems of this native rush, which grows to 18 inches (45 cm). Confine roots to a container to prevent spreading. Good in flower arrangements. Zone 5.

❧ DWARF CATTAIL (*Typha laxmanni*) — at 3 feet (1 m), this is a good short alternative to the tall common cattail, with the same brown summer catkins. Like all cattails, however, it is very invasive, so plant in a container. Zone 5.

❧ DWARF JAPANESE SWEET FLAG (*Acorus gramineus*) — from the arum family, this dainty grassy plant grows about 18 inches (45 cm) tall. There is an excellent, showy yellow-striped form, *A. gramineus* 'Variegatus'. Zone 5.

❧ GRACEFUL CATTAIL OR NARROW-LEAF CATTAIL (*Typha angustifolia*) — at 6 feet (2 m), still a tall cattail but its narrow, elegant foliage distinguishes it from the common variety. Restrain roots in containers to curb spreading. Do not remove foliage from any cattails (or bulrushes) until spring, to let plants breathe. Zone 4.

❧ FLOWERING RUSH (*Butomus umbellatus*) — one of the best flowering marginals, with 3- to 4-foot (1 to 1.3 m) stems bearing rose-pink flower umbels. Triangular, rush-like leaves start out burgundy, then turn rich green in summer. Zone 6.

❦ LIZARD'S TAIL OR WATER DRAGON (*Saururus cernuus*) — curled, fluffy, white flower spikes are fragrant, long-lasting in summer. Handsome, narrow leaves. Zone 6.

❦ PICKEREL RUSH OR PICKERELWEED (*Pontederia cordata*) — long heart-shape leaves and a profusion of intense blue flower spikes rising 2 to 3 feet (60 to 90 cm) from this native plant in mid-summer to fall. Fertilize to encourage continued flowering. Easily grown, and a must for pond gardeners. Zone 5.

Pickerel Rush (Pontederia cordata)

❦ PRIMROSE CREEPER (*Jussiaea diffusa*) — belongs to evening-primrose family. Creeping stems with bright-yellow 2-inch (5 cm) flowers. Shade tolerant. Zone 6.

❦ ROSE MALLOW OR WATER HIBISCUS (*Hibiscus moscheutos* or *H. palustris*) — native to fresh and saltwater marshes of Carolina, Massachusetts, and Florida west to Indiana. Huge pink, red and white hollyhock-like flowers on 6-foot (2 m) stems. Garden selection is *H. moscheutos* 'Southern Belle'. May not overwinter but will

Rose Mallow (Hibiscus moscheutos 'Southern Belle')

flower the first year from seed started indoors. Zone 7.

❦ SPIKE RUSH (*Eleocharis montevidensis*) — low, dense plant with quilled, rush-like leaves and brown spiky summer flowers. Height is about 8 to 12 inches (22 to 30 cm) but varies according to depth of planting. Zone 5.

❦ SWEET FLAG (*Acorus calamus*) — native to Asia but naturalized in North America. Leaves emit a sweet lemony scent. Sword-like foliage and textured gold flower spadix. Grows 2 to 4 feet (60 to 120 cm) tall. To prevent mildew, plant in full sun. Wear gloves when cutting; sweet flag has been known to cause a skin rash. Variegated form is *A. calamus* 'Variegatus'. Zone 4.

❦ WATER PLANTAIN (*Alisma plantago-aquatica*) — young foliage of this native plant is ribbon-like, but older ribbed leaves float on surface. Pale-pink flowers on 2- to 3-foot (60 to 90 cm) stems in summer. Flowers best in shallow water. Zone 5.

❦ YELLOW WATER IRIS (*I. pseudacorus*) — reliable and elegant to 4 feet (1.3 m), the big yellow spring

flower of this naturalized European is the fleur-de-lys on the French coat of arms. Vigorous; will grow in shallow water or moist garden soil. Yellow-green variegated form is *I. pseudacorus* 'Variegata'. Zone 4.

For Planting 6 Inches (15 cm) Deep

❦ BOGBEAN (*Menyanthes trifoliata*) — very hardy native marsh plant that spreads by rhizomes. Bean-like leaves and fragrant, starry, white flowers with stems that creep over water. Good for disguising edges of artificial ponds. Zone 5.

❦ BULRUSH (*Scirpus validus*) — sometimes confused with cattail, but bears flat-topped spiky brown flowers, not catkins. This native sedge is common in sunny marshes and shallow water to 3 feet (1 m). Bulrushes are being tested as natural biological cleansers at industrial sites with contaminated run-off. Somewhat invasive, so best grown in container in pond. Zone 5.

❦ FLOATING HEART OR WATER FRINGE (*Nymphoides peltata*) — stoliniferous, with purple-mottled, round leaves and frilly yellow flowers rising 2 inches (5 cm) above

Floating Heart (Nymphoides peltata)

the water. Vigorous; needs periodic thinning. Will root in mud; tolerates depths up to 20 inches (50 cm). Good fish fry habitat. Zone 5.

Melon Sword (Echinodorus cordifolius)

❦ MELON SWORD (*Echinodorus cordifolius*) — native from Illinois to southern United States. Long, upright leaves; white flowers on whorled stems become prostrate on the water. Zone 6.

❦ SPEARWORT OR TONGUE BUTTERCUP (*Ranunculus lingua*) — stolon-forming aquatic buttercup, with erect stems bearing golden-yellow flowers from June to August. Adapts to water from 2 to 12 inches (5 to 30 cm) deep. Zone 5.

❦ WATER CLOVER, PEPPERWORT, WATER SHAMROCK (*Marsilea* spp.) — European and Asian aquatic fern that has naturalized and is hardy in parts of eastern North America. Four-part shamrock-like leaves float in 6- to 8-inch (15 to 20 cm) deep water, but will stand erect in shallower water. Zone 5.

❦ WHITE RUSH (*Scirpus lacustris* ssp. *tabernaemontani* 'Albescens') — pale green-and-yellow-striped bulrush, growing to 6 feet (2 m). Better for gardens than common bulrush. Zone 5.

❦ ZEBRA RUSH (*Scirpus lacustris* ssp. *tabernaemontani* 'Zebrinus') — quill-like stems, banded green and white, become greener as summer progresses. Grows 1 to 3 feet (30 to 90 cm) tall. Zone 6.

Zebra Rush (Scirpus lacustris *ssp.* tabernaemontani *'Zebrinus'*)

Tropical/Tender Marginal Aquatics

Most tropical aquatics are treated as annuals in garden ponds but a few, such as umbrella palm and papyrus, can be wintered indoors as houseplants.

For Planting *at* Water Level

❦ BOG LILY OR SWAMP LILY (*Crinum americanum*) — native to marshes and slow streams in southern United States. Has sweet-scented, spidery white flowers on 2-foot (60 cm) stems in July and August.

❦ GREEN TARO OR ELEPHANT'S EAR (*Colocasia escuelenta*) — grows to height of between 2 and 3 feet (60 to 90 cm), with yellow, rank-smelling arum flowers in hot summers.

❦ IMPERIAL TARO (*Colocasia antiquorum illustris*) — thick stems to 3-1/2 feet (105 cm) and dark-blotched long, oval leaves. Makes a good houseplant.

❦ MONKEY FLOWER OR MONKEY MUSK (*Mimulus guttatus*) — found from Mexico to Alaska. Showy yellow flowers; self-seeds prolifically and can be relied upon to return year after year, even in colder climates. Good in a bog.

❦ TROPICAL WATER CANNA (*C. aquatica*) — similar to garden canna. Large, elliptical leaves, with long-blooming orange-yellow flowers. Many good peach, red and pink cultivars.

❦ UMBRELLA PALM (*Cyperus alternifolius*) — very popular tropical aquatic in naturalistic ponds, and an excellent centerpiece in a formal pond. Stems bear palm-like umbels of spiky flowers. Grows about 2.5 feet (75 cm) tall, but taller forms are available. Dwarf form is *C. alternifolius gracilis* which, at 12 to 18 inches (30 to 45 cm) tall, is a good choice for a tub garden.

PEBBLE POOLS *and* BUBBLE FOUNTAINS

These are effective low-maintenance water features, similar in principle to wall fountains, and are ideal for a patio or terrace. They're also a safe way to include water in a garden where there are small children.

❦ To make a pebble pool, start by digging out a small below-ground reservoir, then line it with flexible pond liner or fit it with a watertight container.

❦ Place a small submersible pump in the water, then plug it into a nearby grounded outlet. Attach a length of flexible tubing to the pump outlet and bring its end to the surface.

❦ Cover the excavation with a metal grate and thread the tubing through it. Pile smooth river rocks on top of the grate, pulling the tubing end to the upper surface of the rocks but making sure it isn't visible.

❦ When the pump is turned on, the water flows up through the rocks, bubbling up and splashing over them before cascading back into the reservoir.

❦ An old millstone makes an attractive bubble fountain, substituting for the river rocks mentioned above. Thread the tubing from the pump in the reservoir below, through the millstone's axle hole (which should be caulked at the surface to prevent water from seeping back down through it).

❦ Place the millstone atop the metal grate. When the pump is turned on, the water flows over the surface of the millstone, spilling over the sides and returning to the reservoir. If the millstone has a slight lip, the water will pool on the surface before spilling over the sides.

*Horsetail rush (*Equisetum spp.*), an invasive plant in open water, takes on a very architectural appearance in a container, which also curbs its aggressive tendencies.*

CONTAINER WATER GARDENS

It isn't necessary to excavate a pond in your garden in order to have water lilies or goldfish. Any watertight container can become a portable lily or fish pond. Provided you empty breakable containers in winter to prevent frost-cracking, this mini garden is remarkably easy to maintain.

❦ Potential containers include Oriental ginger or pickling jars, colorful ceramic or porcelain pots, basins, urns and even plastic planters. Wooden half whiskey barrels are inexpensive and have a rustic look; they can be lined with a flexible pond liner or fitted with a rigid fiberglass shell designed specifically for half-barrels. A container can be placed above ground or, for an interesting pond-like effect, sunk partially below it.

❦ Small hardy water lilies perfect for containers are yellow 'Pygmaea Helvola', white *Nymphaea tetragona* and bronze-orange 'Graziella'. 'Dauben' is a diminutive blue tropical lily that thrives in only a few inches of water. Dwarf cultivars of the sacred lotus, such as *Nelumbo* 'Momo Botan', are perfect for a half whiskey barrel, which is large enough for a few additional plants that can be raised to the appropriate depth on brick piers.

❦ Even without aquatic plants or fish, a handsome container filled with still water that reflects the sky and trees above adds an evocative, tranquil air to any garden setting.

POND MAINTENANCE THROUGH *the* SEASONS

SPRING

❧ It is not always necessary to clean out the pond. Very large ponds with thriving ecosystems seldom need cleaning, but small ponds with lots of plants usually need a partial water change and cleaning out in spring or fall.

❧ Gardeners who leave water lilies and fish to overwinter in deep water outdoors may choose to do maintenance in spring, as they divide aquatic plants and check on the condition of the fish. Others may wish to tidy the pond in autumn as they scoop out fallen leaves.

❧ If your pond exudes a foul odor and the water is dark when the ice melts in spring, there is a problem with rotting vegetation. Start by pumping approximately two-thirds of the volume out into adjacent flower beds, lawn or bog garden. If you used a de-icer through the winter, remove it. Remove fish and aquatic plants to a holding tank filled with the old pond water. Drain the rest of the water, removing debris with a sieve or wet-vac. Don't scrub pond walls too clean; they should retain some of their brown algae coating.

❧ Check that edging and waterfall rocks are still in alignment and that the liner at these points is cushioned with protective underlay.

❧ Flush out pumps, hoses and filters, and fill the pond with clean water, adding a dechlor agent if fish and plants are being held in temporary containment. The biofilter will take 4 to 5 weeks to establish nitrifying bacteria.

❧ Divide rootbound water lilies and aquatic plants, changing the soil and adding fertilizer tablets, if desired.

❧ Check water quality with a pond-testing kit before returning fish from the holding tank. If fish have been kept in an indoor aquarium during winter, put them in the pond only when the water temperature has reached 15°C (60°F), and

acclimatize them slowly to the new water. Do not feed them until the water temperature reaches 18°C (64°F).

❧ When the water temperature reaches 15°C (60°F), hardy water lilies may be planted; wait until the water temperature reaches 20°C (70°F) before planting tropical water lilies. Start tropicals at 4 inches (10 cm) under the water surface, hardys 6 to 8 inches (15 to 20 cm), lowering them to their correct depth as water warms and new foliage reaches the water surface.

SUMMER

❧ Remove dead leaves and flowers from water lilies and fertilize every 4 weeks or when lily flowers or leaves become small, or new foliage has a yellowish look.

❧ Continue to monitor water quality with a pond-testing kit, especially during hot weather. If fish are seen gasping at the surface, increase oxygenation with an air pump.

❧ Replenish water lost through evaporation by spraying it in with a hose. Try not to replace more than

Sarracenia purpurea, 62
Saururus cernuus, 79
Scirpus lacustris ssp.
     tabernaemontani
     'Albernia', 80
   S. l. ssp. tabernaemontani
     'Zebrinus', 80, 80
   S. validus, 79
Sedges, 47
Sedums, 56
Serviceberries, 47
Shrub swamps, 62
Shrubs, 47, 56, 63
Shubunkins, 82
Siberian iris, 56
Silver maple, 62
Site considerations, 15-17
Skinner's brome, 56
Snails, 31, 77
Spearwort, 80
Sphagnum moss, 60
Spider lily, 81
Spike rush, 62, 79
Spiked water milfoil, 81
Spireas, 56
Spruce, 56
Stephanandra, 41
Stepping stones, 11
Stringweed, 30
Submerged oxygenating
     plants, 68
Submersible pumps, 22,
     50, 85
Subsoil, 36
Sumac, 47
Summersweet, 47
Sumps, 17
Sunlight, 15, 22
Surfacing plants, 68
Swamp birch, 60
Swamp lily, 80
Swamp milkweed, 77
Swamps, 62
Sweet flag, 17, 62, 68, 79

T

Tadpoles, 31
Tamarack, 47, 60, 62
Tap water, 87
Terrace, 85
Thalia dealbata, 81
Thorn trees, 47
Thyme, 56
Tongue buttercup, 80
Topography, 17
Toxic ammonia, 25
Toxic gases, 87
Toxic plants, 17
Tree swamps, 62
Trees, 17, 45, 47, 60
Trembling aspen, 47
Tropical water canna, 80
Tropical water lilies, 86, 87
Tropical/tender marginal
     aquatics, 80
Trumpet vine, 45
Tsukabai, 11
Typha angustifolia, 78
   T. latifolia, 78, 78
   T. laxmanni, 78
   T. minima, 77

U

Umbrella palm, 80
Underlay, 38, 39, 41, 54, 59
Utility cables, 17

V

Vaccinium corymbosum, 60
   V. oxycoccum, 60
Vallisneria americana, 31, 76
Variegated manna grass, 78
Venus's Vale, 11
Versailles, gardens, 11
Villa d'Este, 11
Vines, 45
Virginia creeper, 45

W

Walkways, 44
Wall fountains, 9, 84,
     84, 85
Water canna, 81
Water clover, 80
Water dragon, 79
Water features, 84
Water fern, 76
Water forget-me-not, 78, 78
Water fringe, 79, 79
Water hawthorn, 81
Water hibiscus, 79
Water hyacinth, 30, 30, 68,
     76, 76, 87
Water iris, 47, 69
Water lettuce, 68, 76, 87
Water lilies, 4, 9, 15, 22, 28,
     30, 31, 36, 40, 68, 69,
     85, 86
   'Dauben', 85
   'Graziella', 85
   'Pygmaea Helvola', 85
   growing, 70
   hardy, 71, 72, 74, 85
   miniature, 10
   Nymphaea tetragona, 85
   overwintering, 35, 72
   planting, 70-71, 70-71
   pygmy, 19
   tropical, 72, 74
Water meal, 77
Water parsley, 81
Water plaintain, 79
Water poppy, 77, 77
Water quality testing kit, 86
Water shamrock, 80
Water velvet, 76
Water wall, 50
Water ornaments
     pump-dependent, 17
Water
   hardness, 25
   acidity, 25
   alkalinity, 25

Waterfalls, 17, 25, 34, 36,
     38, 56
   aesthetics, 10
   construction, 50
   ecology, 50
   lined, from pond
     subsoil, 54
   plants, 56
   prefabricated stone units,
     50, 50
   problems, 53
   pumps, 50, 54
   site and design
     considerations, 53
Waterfowl, 83
Waterweed, 76
Weeping tiles, 17
Weeping trees, 45
Weeping willow, 47
White cedar, 62
White pine, 45
White rush, 80
White water snowflake,
     81, 81
Wild celery, 76
Wildlife, 34
Willow, 62
Winds, 15
Winterberry, 47
Wiring, 17, 44
Wolffia spp., 77

Y

Yatsubashi, 11
Yellow flag iris, 17
Yellow pond lily, 17, 76
Yellow water iris, 79
Yellow water lily, 76
Yellow water snowflake, 81
Yew, 45

Z

Zebra rush, 59, 80, 80
Zeolite, 27

EDITORIAL DIRECTOR   Hugh Brewster

PROJECT EDITOR   Wanda Nowakowska

EDITORIAL ASSISTANCE   Rebecca Hanes-Fox

PRODUCTION DIRECTOR   Susan Barrable

PRODUCTION COORDINATOR   Sandra L. Hall

BOOK DESIGN AND LAYOUT   Gordon Sibley Design Inc.

PRINTING AND BINDING   Tien Wah Press

CANADIAN GARDENING'S
WATER *in the* GARDEN
was produced by
Madison Press Books